# DK eyewonder

# Vikings

Written and edited by Carrie Love and Lorrie Mack
Designed by Penny Lamprell, Sadie Thomas,
Tory Gordon-Harris, and Clare Shedden
Managing art editor Rachael Foster
Picture researcher Liz Moore
Production Sarah Jenkins
DTP designer Ben Hung
Illustrator Andy Cooke
Jacket designer Mary Sandberg
Jacket editor Mariza O'Keeffe
Consultant Angus Konstam

Wherever the Vikings lived, experts have built reconstructions of their homes and farms, and people dress up as Vikings to re-create their way of life. To bring the Viking world alive, we have used pictures of these reconstructions in this book. Thanks to Murton Park, York, England, for allowing us to take photos of their re-construction of a Viking village.

**REVISED EDITION**
**DK UK**
Senior editor Caroline Stamps
Senior art editor Rachael Grady
Jacket editor Manisha Majithia
Jacket design Nishesh Batnagar, Mark Cavanagh
Jacket design development manager
Sophia M Tampakopoulos Turner
Producer (print production) Mary Slater
Producer (pre-production) Rachel Ng
Publisher Andrew Macintyre

**DK INDIA**
Senior editor Shatarupa Chaudhuri
Art editor Shipra Jain
Managing editor Alka Thakur Hazarika
Managing art editor Romi Chakraborty
DTP designer Dheeraj Singh
Picture researcher Sumedha Chopra

First published in Great Britain in 2007
This edition published in Great Britain in 2016 by
Dorling Kindersley Limited
80 Strand, London WC2R 0RL

Copyright © 2007, © 2016 Dorling Kindersley Limited
A Penguin Random House Company

16 17 18 19 20 10 9 8 7 6 5 4 3 2 1
001 – 196639 – 02/2016

A CIP catalogue record for this book
is available from the British Library.
ISBN: 978-1-4093-4424-7

Printed and bound in China

# Contents

# Meet the Vikings

More than a thousand years ago, from the eighth to eleventh centuries, the Vikings set out to explore and raid countries across the world. Vikings came from Scandinavia – Norway, Sweden, and Denmark.

## Mystery man

The Vikings didn't paint or draw, but they were great carvers and modellers. This small silver head may be a god, a hero, or a warrior.

GREENLAND

ICELAND

ATLANTIC OCEAN

NORTH AMERICA

*Follow the arrows and take an ocean voyage with the Vikings.*

## Exploring the world

In their fine ships, the Vikings explored, raided, and traded across Europe, Russia, and the Middle East. They even got as far as Iceland, Greenland, and North America.

LABRADOR

NEWFOUNDLAND

### Viking words

**Viking** From *vikingr*, an old Norwegian word for "sea raider".

**Thing** Local assembly, where people could exchange ideas.

**Karl, jarl, thrall** Free person, noble person, slave.

**Skald** Composer of poems about kings and heroes.

This map
shows the
routes many
Vikings may
have travelled.

Homelands

Settlements

## Masters of craft

Vikings were not just brilliant sailors
and fighters – they were also skilled
craftspeople who made beautiful jewellery,
textiles, metalwork, and furniture.

RUSSIA

FINLAND

*Elaborate
oval brooch
worked in gold.*

*Helmets were
made from
iron plates
welded together.*

NORWAY

SWEDEN

DENMARK

NORTH
SEA

*Skilled
blacksmiths
made strong,
sharp swords.*

EUROPE

BRITISH
ISLES

FRANCE

## Mighty warriors

Fast and fierce
in attack, Viking
warriors were feared
everywhere. With
strength and speed
on their side, they
launched violent
raids on rich
towns, farms,
and monasteries.

# Ruling the sea

The Vikings were skilled sailors.
Their well-built warships and
longships carried them on
dangerous voyages through
rough seas, hidden rocks,
and jagged icebergs.

*This is an artist's impression of a Viking
warship with a mythical beast as a figurehead.*

## Versatile vessels

Viking longships – the longest and
fastest Viking warships – were special
as they could be rowed or sailed.
Vikings used the oars to row
through rivers
and coastal
waters. The
large sail helped
them get through
open waters.

### ARE WE THERE YET?

The Vikings had no form of compass so they navigated by
staying close to land when they could, or by using the Sun
and stars to work out their position. The Vikings learnt from
experience and passed on information from one generation to
the next. They had a good knowledge of fish, seabirds, wind,
and wave patterns, which helped them to steer in the right
direction and survive at sea.

## Brilliant boats

Vikings made a range of ships and boats for various purposes. There were warships (usually longships), ferries (which carried passengers across rivers and fjords), small rowing boats (used on lakes), cargo ships, and fishing boats.

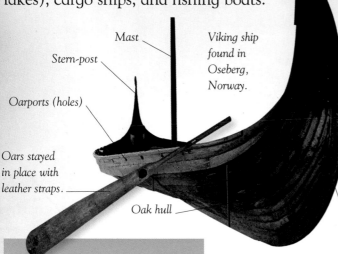

*This prow ends with a snake's head in a spiral.*

Mast

Stern-post

Oarports (holes)

*Viking ship found in Oseberg, Norway.*

*Intricate carvings of animals*

Oars stayed in place with leather straps.

Oak hull

*Strakes (planks) of wood were overlapped in a technique called "clinker" boat-building.*

*Viking ships were adaptable and fast. They were also easy to navigate through narrow and shallow rivers.*

## Valued heritage

Viking carving plays an important role in Scandinavian culture and tourism. This prow adorns a modern sightseeing ship in Stockholm.

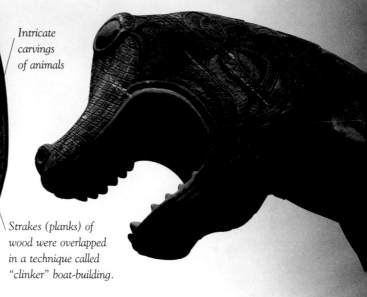

Vikings frightened their enemies with ferocious figureheads.

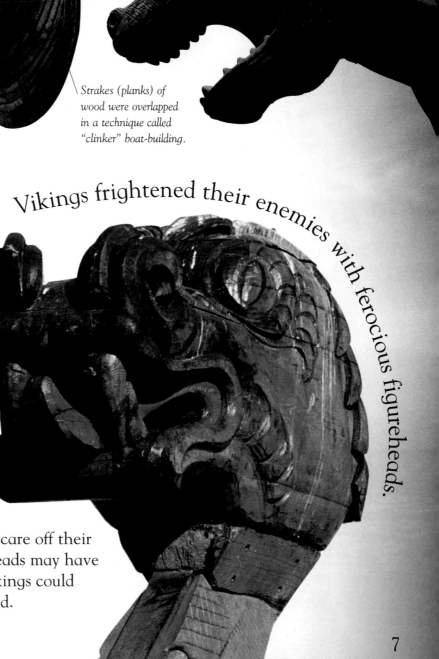

## Scary heads

The Vikings often carved figureheads of beasts and dragons on their ship prows to scare off their enemies. Some wooden figureheads may have been detachable so that the Vikings could position them before they landed.

# Daring discoveries

Using their superb skills as shipbuilders and navigators, the Vikings set off across the ocean to find new lands to colonize and farm. The Vikings landed in North America, centuries before Christopher Columbus. They also discovered Iceland and Greenland.

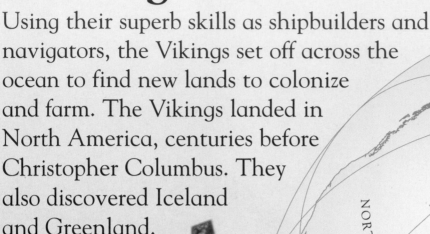

NORTH AMERICA

Greenland

Iceland

### Searching for something

Vikings explored the world for many reasons. Accused of murder, the famous Erik the Red was forced to leave Iceland, so he fled to Greenland where he settled. Others (mainly from Norway) left in search of land to farm, as their home countries had become overcrowded.

*Sea voyages were long and dangerous!*

## Territorial facts

**Greenland** Not very green, it's mostly snow and ice.

**Iceland** In good conditions it took seven days to get from Scandinavia to Iceland.

**Newfoundland** Remains of the Viking settlement here were only discovered in 1960.

## Land of ice

The Vikings discovered Iceland in 870 CE. The inner area of the land is hard to inhabit, with its mountains, glaciers, and active volcanoes. Settlements were built around the coast because it was green and fertile – by 930 CE many people lived there.

*This was the site where the Althing (see page 31) met in Iceland.*

*Statue in Iceland of Leif the Lucky (see below), who was Erik the Red's son.*

## What's in a name?

By choosing Greenland as the name for the snowy country he explored, Erik the Red encouraged people to move there. As a result, Vikings established two large settlements in areas that were good for farming. They raised sheep and cattle, but relied on seals and reindeer for food.

*Viking ruins in Greenland*

## A new world

Leif the Lucky was the first European to set foot in North America. His Viking colony in Newfoundland is not just the oldest European settlement in the New World – it's the only one.

*Reconstruction of a Viking settlement in L'Anse aux Meadows, Newfoundland (modern Canada).*

# The Viking terror

Travelling Vikings not only discovered new territories, but also invaded towns, cities, and smaller settlements throughout Europe. They attacked from the sea or sailed up rivers in search of treasure they could carry off. Sometimes, they even demanded huge payments to leave.

*This 14th-century manuscript shows the Viking invasion of Britain several centuries earlier.*

*Warriors attacking from the sea could raid, loot, and sail away before the local ruler could arrive to protect his townspeople.*

**Smash and grab**
Bands of Vikings usually arrived by ship to attack farms, churches, and monasteries by surprise. They then plundered them for valuables, money, and slaves.

*Viking marauders were carved on this gravestone at Lindisfarne monastery.*

## Holy ruins

The monastery on the holy island of Lindisfarne (off northeast England) was raided repeatedly by Vikings who, in 793 CE, slaughtered the monks and stole their treasures. Today, only its ruins remain.

## Paris under siege

This Victorian illustration brings to life a violent Viking attack on Paris in 865 CE, led by a chieftain called Rollo.

*Viking longships were built to navigate shallow waters and land on flat shorelines.*

*This bishop's cross from Ireland was taken to Sweden by Vikings.*

*These coins date from the period of Viking rule in Ireland.*

## Victory in Ireland

The Vikings began to raid Ireland in 795 CE, and by the 820s they had worked their way around the coast and moved inland. Dublin became first a base from which to attack the rest of the country, then a busy Viking centre for trade with other lands.

### Attack facts

● Some Vikings who raided northern France settled there. The area became known as Normandy – "land of north men".

● One Viking band took 62 ships to Spain, Italy, and Africa.

● The Vikings first began to raid at the end of the 700s.

# Weapons and warriors

Vikings were daring and courageous at war, following their lord or king into any conflict. Warriors believed that honour and glory in battle lasted forever, even beyond death. Their most prized possessions – their weapons – were often buried with them.

## Warrior god

In this engraving Tyr, Viking god of heroic combat, wears a bear's head as a helmet and a bearskin cloak.

## Symbols of power

Great leaders carried weapons with precious and intricate decoration that showed their importance. This iron axehead is inlaid with silver wire.

*Viking swords were double-edged – both edges of the blade were sharpened.*

*The end of a sword is called a pommel.*

*Spearhead from Denmark*

*Broad axe blade*

*Viking shields were round and made of wood, like this replica used in re-enactments.*

## Men of iron

Viking weapons were made of iron, sometimes decorated with copper or silver. To make sharp steel edges, carbon was added to the iron when it was hot.

## Horse power

While early warriors fought on foot, later Vikings were skilled horsemen. This silver figure dates from the 10th century.

## Battle grounds

Viking warfare was brutal and bloody. Warriors saw battle as a noble pursuit, and those who proved themselves were often rewarded with land and riches.

## HORNS NOT REQUIRED

We think of Viking warriors as wearing scary horned helmets, but there's little evidence to support this image – few examples survive, and experts think these were used for religious rituals. During the 1800s, Romantic artists first portrayed Vikings with horns, and it's their pictures that keep the myth alive.

VIKING AUDITION

No horns!

*Vikings usually won their battles by surprise attack. In new lands, they would arrive by boat, strike on foot, then return to their ship.*

Ramparts — River — Four houses around a square yard — Ditches — Cemetery — Extra rampart — Road — Workshops and houses

# Living in a fort

Around 980 CE, the Vikings built four large circular forts (Aggersborg, Fyrkat, Trelleborg, and Nonebakken) in Denmark. Historians think King Harald Bluetooth ordered their construction to show his rule and symbolize his power.

## Adding on

Trelleborg differed slightly from the other forts – it had 15 houses outside the main ramparts, protected by an extra rampart.

*The layout of a Viking fort was geometric, and circular ramparts made of earth, turf, and wood kept enemies out.*

*Trelleborg (shown above) was 136 m (445 ft) across.*

## Building the past

At Fyrkat fort, a Viking house has been carefully re-created. Its main door leads into a small entrance area. This opens onto a huge central living space.

## The mighty sword

At Trelleborg, people re-enact scenes from Viking life. Here, warriors use swords for fierce hand-to-hand combat. Real Vikings gave their weapons names such as "leg-biter" or "killer". Those who were wealthy had their swords decorated on the hilt (handle).

*Viking shields were made from wood with metal or leather rims.*

*The tiny notch in this arrowhead is designed to cut feathers for the end of arrows.*

*Smiths are craftsmen who work with metal. This smith is hammering sharp heads for the tips of arrows.*

## Hard at work

At Fyrkat fort, two longhouses were used as "smithies" – workshops where smiths made weapons and jewellery from iron, silver, and gold.

*Viking forts also had carpentry workshops.*

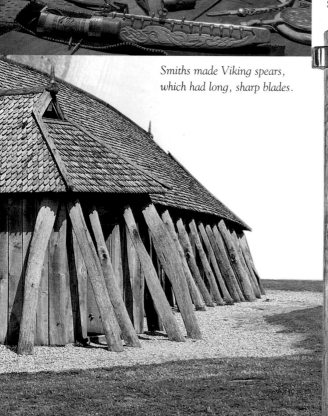

*Smiths made Viking spears, which had long, sharp blades.*

*The most popular Viking weapons were axes with long wooden handles.*

15

# Home life

Viking houses were usually rectangular, and large enough to house more than one generation of a family. Poor people had few possessions and little luxury, but wealthy homes might feature wooden furniture and decorative wall panels.

## Practical solutions

Building materials varied around the Viking world. Turf (above), bark, or thatch (below) were used for the roof if timber was unavailable.

*Thatch is made from straw.*

## Domestic facts

● Women were in charge of the family's valuables.

● In most homes, everyone slept in the same room. Rich people, though, had a separate room from their servants.

● Houses were lit with torches made from bundles of straw.

## Wild walls

Some Viking houses had a traditional wattle-and-daub construction. The woven branches that form the basic structure are called wattle.

*Daub, a mixture of clay and dung, coated the wattle to seal it.*

## The basic plan

Most Viking houses had a single central living room. People sat and slept on raised platforms lining the walls. This reconstruction is partly finished – the wattle is in place, but not the daub.

## Lock it up

Vikings didn't have much furniture, but they kept their valuables in locked chests. Keys were symbols of responsibility.

*Ninth-century bronze key found in Denmark*

## The hearth of the home

Vikings ate, drank, and socialized around a raised stone hearth on the stamped earth floor. The fire was needed for warmth, for cooking, and for light.

# Getting dressed

Men wore either round or peaked hats. Some peaked hats had silver ornaments at the top.

For every day, Vikings wore clothes made from plain wool. Tunics and dresses may have had woven, coloured borders. The very rich wore clothes decorated with gold and silver thread.

Most Viking brooches were oval in shape.

## Perfect miniatures

Viking children looked like small versions of their parents. Boys wore tunics over trousers and girls wore dresses and aprons.

Vikings kept their hair tidy with combs that were very much like ours, except they were carved from bone.

## An eye for fashion

Viking women wore long under-dresses with aprons on top. Men wore long, tunic-like shirts over woollen trousers, often with a cloak. Both men and women used brooches; women had two to fasten their aprons, and men had one to fasten their cloaks.

Both poor and rich wore leather shoes, usually made of goatskin.

# The well-dressed warrior

Wealthy warriors wore heavy leather or chain-mail tunics and metal helmets. Their cloaks were arranged to keep the fighting arm free. The strap that carried their sword was called a baldric.

Chain mail is woven from thousands of iron links, each one forged separately.

Chain mail was very heavy, but flexible.

This iron helmet has a noseguard and a band of chain mail at the back to protect the warrior's neck.

High-ranking warriors wore wolfskin.

Leather belt with bronze buckle

# Fighting from the ranks

When they went to war for their local noble or chieftain, peasants had no protective clothing. They carried a weapon – an axe or a spear – and a wooden shield.

Peasants were freemen, not slaves. Most were farmers.

Axe

Shield

Viking warriors were unlike modern soldiers: they didn't have a uniform. Every man had to provide his own clothes and weapons.

19

# Viking jewellery

Viking men and women loved jewellery – they wore rings, brooches, bracelets, and necklaces. The poor made their jewellery from bronze, pewter, or bone, whereas the rich used silver and gold.

*Images from mythology often decorate Viking jewellery. This etched pendant takes its shape from Thor's hammer.*

## Followers of fashion

Vikings tended to adapt designs from other countries. This huge dress pin (which was more for display than practicality) was based on a style the Vikings saw in the British Isles.

*Silver pin and ring, inlaid with gold*

This intricate brooch was made from sheet gold pressed into a lead die.

*Vikings used the black compound niello (made from silver, copper, and lead) for engraving.*

### Shining symbols

● Vikings displayed their status with the jewellery they wore.

● Kings rewarded successful raiders with precious jewellery.

● Valuables were buried underground in hoards. The largest ever found contained 40 kg (88 lb) of silver.

## Practical purposes

Vikings didn't have buttons or zips – everything that couldn't be tied or belted was fastened with a pin or a brooch.

*Hoop and heart detailing were added using twisted gold wire and filled in with extra blobs of the precious metal.*

## Around their necks

Gold, silver, amber, and glass were used for Viking bead necklaces. Pendants may have been worn on chains or strips of leather. Viking neck-rings were sometimes made by melting down silver Arab coins.

Considered valuable, beads were gathered up during raids. Vikings could also buy beads in their own markets.

*Necklace made of glass beads*

*Craftsmen melted down broken glass to make bright beads.*

*This necklace is made of boar tusks, amber, and glass beads. Animal bones left over from cooking were often used to make jewellery.*

## Rings everywhere

Only Swedish women wore earrings, but male and female Vikings from all over wore rings on their fingers, arms, and neck. Gold, jet, coloured glass, and amber were all used to make finger-rings.

*Men and women both wore finger-rings.*

*The fine decoration on this gold arm-ring was applied with a stamp.*

# Living off the land

Although their land was often barren and overcrowded, Vikings relied on farming for their food. As a result, some people moved to faraway lands in search of fertile soil and bigger farms for their crops and animals.

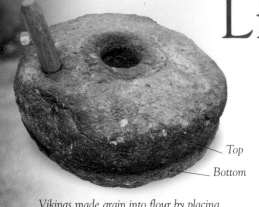

Top

Bottom

*Vikings made grain into flour by placing it between the two halves of a quern stone, then turning a wooden handle to grind the top against the bottom.*

## Jarlshof farm

When it was built, this ruined ninth-century Viking farmhouse in Scotland had two rooms – a main hall and a kitchen. The farmer and his family would have slept on platforms against the wall.

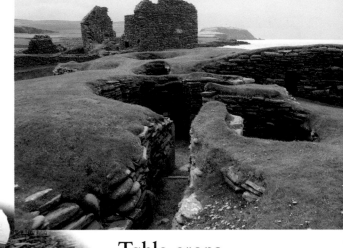

## Table crops

As well as gathering wild vegetables, Vikings grew them on the land. They ate vegetables that grew well in cool climates, such as carrots, parsnips, turnips, wild celery, leeks, onions, peas, and cabbages

**Useful beasts**
Vikings raised cattle for their meat and their hide, but mostly for their milk, which was used to make butter and cheese.

**Useful tool**
Vikings cut cloth, sheared sheep, and trimmed their beards with shears like these.

*Vikings made clothes and bedding from sheep's wool.*

# Making meals

To cook their food and warm their houses, Vikings kept fires burning all day, which made their homes very smoky. Families ate their main meal in the evening, after sunset.

### On the fire

Food was cooked in cauldrons over an open fire. These pots, made from iron or soapstone, were suspended from a hook on a three-legged stand, or tripod.

### Fishy facts

People in coastal areas depended on seafood for much of their diet. Those who lived inland ate freshwater fish.

*Fish was dried to preserve it through the winter.*

### Pots of clay

Early Vikings mostly used wooden containers for food but later on, clay pots were common. The holes in this round pot show where a patch was once stuck over the crack.

24

## Varied diet

As well as fish and meat, Vikings ate eggs, vegetables, and fruit such as berries. They used herbs to season soups and stews.

## Daily bread

Most Vikings ate bread made from barley rather than wheat flour, and baked over a fire on a griddle. Rich people ate wheat-flour bread baked in an oven.

*Game birds, such as duck, were caught in traps or hunted with short arrows.*

## Fair game

As well as hares, Vikings trapped and hunted deer, bears, elk, wild boars, reindeer, whales, and seals for food.

### Food words

**Cauldron** A huge pot for cooking food over a fire.

**Griddle** A flat metal plate used as a cooking surface.

**Preserve** To stop food from going bad.

**Season** To flavour food with herbs and spices.

# Super skills

The incredible success of the Viking race was largely due to their craft skills. They made strong, fast ships, sharp weapons, beautiful jewellery, durable clothes, and sturdy wooden tools and household items.

*Carved warrior from a ninth-century wooden sledge*

*Like real Viking looms, this replica stands against a wall.*

## Masters of wood

As well as making everything from small figures to furniture, Viking carpenters decorated their work with intricate carvings, and sometimes painting too.

*Leather bindings often protected the edges of a warrior's shield.*

## Home weaving

Vikings made cloth on vertical looms. Heavy stone rings kept the up-and-down (or warp) threads straight and tight.

## Lots of leather

Vikings used leather to make shoes, belts, and clothing. Warriors had leather shirts, leather sheaths for their knives, and leather quivers to hold their arrows.

## Basket making
Vikings wove baskets from cane, reeds, and straw, and used them for general household storage.

## Special skills

● Smiths made everything from cauldrons to locks and keys.

● Carpenters knew the best wood to use for a particular object, and how to cut wood to give it maximum strength.

● Both men and women spun wool or flax (linen) into yarn.

# Trade and travel

The Vikings traded across Europe and as far east as Central Asia and Russia. They bought silver, silk, wine, spices, jewellery, glass, and pottery. In return, they sold honey, tin, wheat, wool, wood, iron, fur, leather, fish, and walrus ivory. Everywhere they went, the Vikings bought and sold slaves.

## Northern treasure
From their own lands and from Greenland and Iceland, Vikings took furs, skins, and ivory to trading centres in western Europe.

*These walrus-tusk chess pieces, found on the Isle of Lewis, were probably lost on the way to being sold in England or Scotland.*

## Golden nuggets
Amber (fossilized tree resin) was traded widely – in its rough state or as beads.

## How much?

Small scales like these were used throughout the Viking world to weigh silver and other precious metals. Before coins were used, goods were bought with hack silver.

*Set of trader's scales from Sweden*

## Getting around

The Vikings navigated Russian rivers in boats they carried overland. The rivers were full of rocks and rapids that made travelling difficult, so many people died on these trips.

## A piece of hack

Vikings created "hack silver" by chopping up jewellery and bars of silver. The weight was often more important to the Vikings than the way the silver looked.

*Hack silver*

*Viking traders bought wheat in Britain.*

*Viking coins*

*This bronze Buddha was made in India in the sixth or seventh century. It was found in the Swedish trading centre of Helgo.*

## Goods in return

Coins were in use only during the later Viking age. Before that, goods were bought with pieces of silver, or traded directly for other goods of similar value. Coins were made in large quantities under King Harald Bluetooth in 975 CE.

# Who's who?

In Viking communities, there were three classes of people. At the lowest level were slaves, who were owned by other people. In the middle were freemen, and at the top were the rich nobles, who had lots of land and many servants.

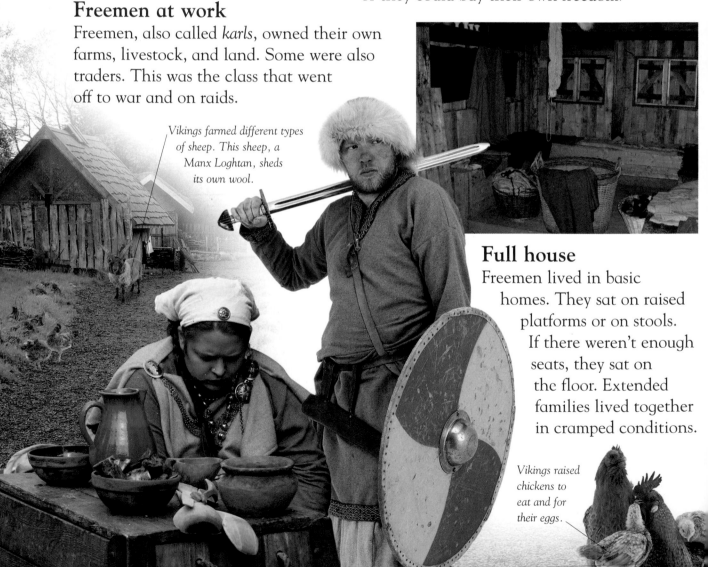

## Slaves

*Thralls* (slaves) were usually captured in other countries. Female slaves cooked, weaved, and ground grain. Male *thralls* did hard labour in the fields. Slaves could be freed by their owners or they could buy their own freedom.

## Freemen at work

Freemen, also called *karls*, owned their own farms, livestock, and land. Some were also traders. This was the class that went off to war and on raids.

*Vikings farmed different types of sheep. This sheep, a Manx Loghtan, sheds its own wool.*

## Full house

Freemen lived in basic homes. They sat on raised platforms or on stools. If there weren't enough seats, they sat on the floor. Extended families lived together in cramped conditions.

*Vikings raised chickens to eat and for their eggs.*

## What is a Thing?

Local assemblies met at a Thing to discuss laws and sort out problems. This stream runs through the site of the Althing in Iceland, where the governing assembly met once a year. Rich nobles and freemen could all have their say at a Thing. Towards the end of the Viking age Norway, Denmark, and Sweden had their own kings, so Things were no longer held.

## The house of a nobleman

The *jarl* class included kings and nobles who could afford large and luxurious homes. Richer Vikings had furniture such as chairs and beds; nobles even had fine tablecloths. The wealthy used imported pottery and jugs.

*The rich drank from glass, pewter, or silver cups as well as drinking horns. The poor used wooden mugs.*

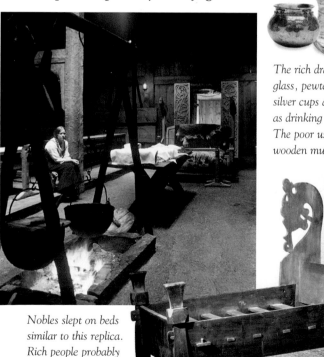

*Nobles slept on beds similar to this replica. Rich people probably slept on mattresses made of feathers.*

### Rags to riches

● *Thralls* wore neck collars to show they weren't free. Female slaves had to keep their hair cut short.

● Nobles used decorated pottery, knives, and spoons.

● "Hundred" was the name for the area governed by a Thing.

# Women and children

Viking women had a lot of power – they could choose their husband and divorce him if he was unfaithful or violent. The wives of freemen and chieftains could voice their opinion in legal or political debates.

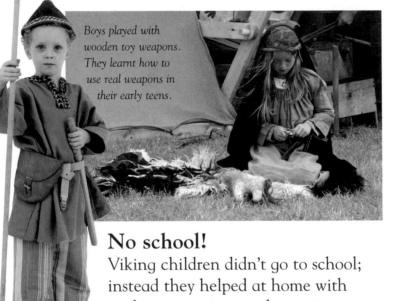

*Boys played with wooden toy weapons. They learnt how to use real weapons in their early teens.*

*Wooden board game*

*Replica of a painted doll*

## No school!
Viking children didn't go to school; instead they helped at home with cooking, weaving, and spinning. They worked in fields and workshops as well.

## Sewing and weaving
Viking mothers often made the clothes for their family, and almost every Viking woman spent part of her day spinning, weaving, or sewing.

*Wool for spinning was collected from sheep.*

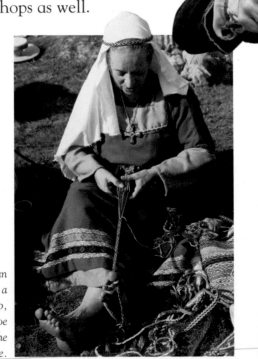

*This woman is braiding a woollen strap, using her toe to keep the braid in place.*

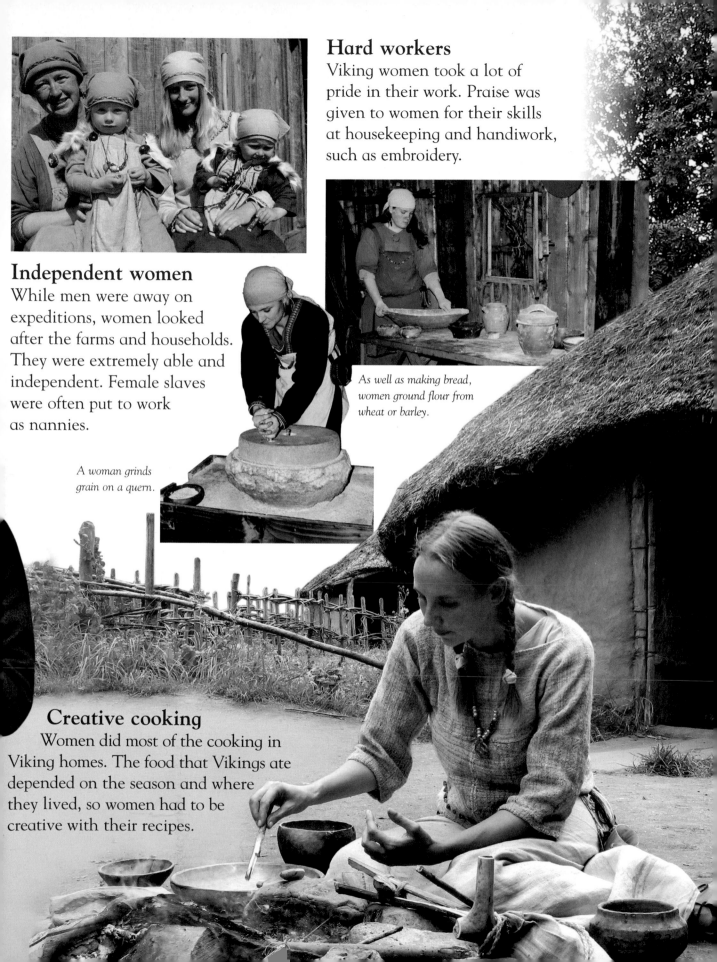

## Hard workers

Viking women took a lot of pride in their work. Praise was given to women for their skills at housekeeping and handiwork, such as embroidery.

As well as making bread, women ground flour from wheat or barley.

## Independent women

While men were away on expeditions, women looked after the farms and households. They were extremely able and independent. Female slaves were often put to work as nannies.

A woman grinds grain on a quern.

## Creative cooking

Women did most of the cooking in Viking homes. The food that Vikings ate depended on the season and where they lived, so women had to be creative with their recipes.

# Fun and games

Vikings enjoyed themselves as much as we do. They held great feasts, where they played music, danced, and told stories. In summer, they went swimming, fishing, and boating, and when winter came, they took to their skates, skis, and sledges.

*This Viking game was called Nine Men's Morris.*

## Winter games

Many winter sports that Vikings engaged in were the same as today. "Ski" is a Norwegian word. People have been skiing in Norway for at least 5,000 years.

*Danish amber gaming piece*

## Board games

Vikings played games scratched onto wood, stone, or leather. Bits of bone or broken crockery were used as counters. Some boards were more elaborate, with decorative carved pieces.

*This illustration shows Ullr, the Viking god of skiing and archery.*

*Vikings called ice skates "ice-legs". To make them, they tied an animal bone to the bottom of a leather boot.*

## Having fun

● Ball games were also popular. Some were a bit like hockey, but they were usually played with a wooden ball.

● Vikings liked to swim, and would compete to see who could stay under water for the longest time.

# Silly dances

Feasts were a time for eating, drinking, and relaxing. Jugglers and jesters entertained guests with tricks and funny dances. Kings had their own poets, called skalds, who performed and praised their ruler.

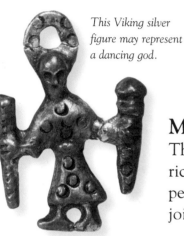

*This Viking silver figure may represent a dancing god.*

*Vikings enjoyed drinking wine, beer, and mead (a honey-based beer) at feasts.*

## Making music

The harp or lyre was played by musicians in rich households while stories were told. Singers performed at feasts and the audience might have joined in to sing a popular folk song or ballad.

*Vikings loved to dance at feasts. Dances ranged from slow to fast and wild.*

*Harpists performed in rich Viking households.*

*Both men and women played music at feasts.*

*This Viking flute was made from a sheep's leg bone. Flutes were played like modern recorders.*

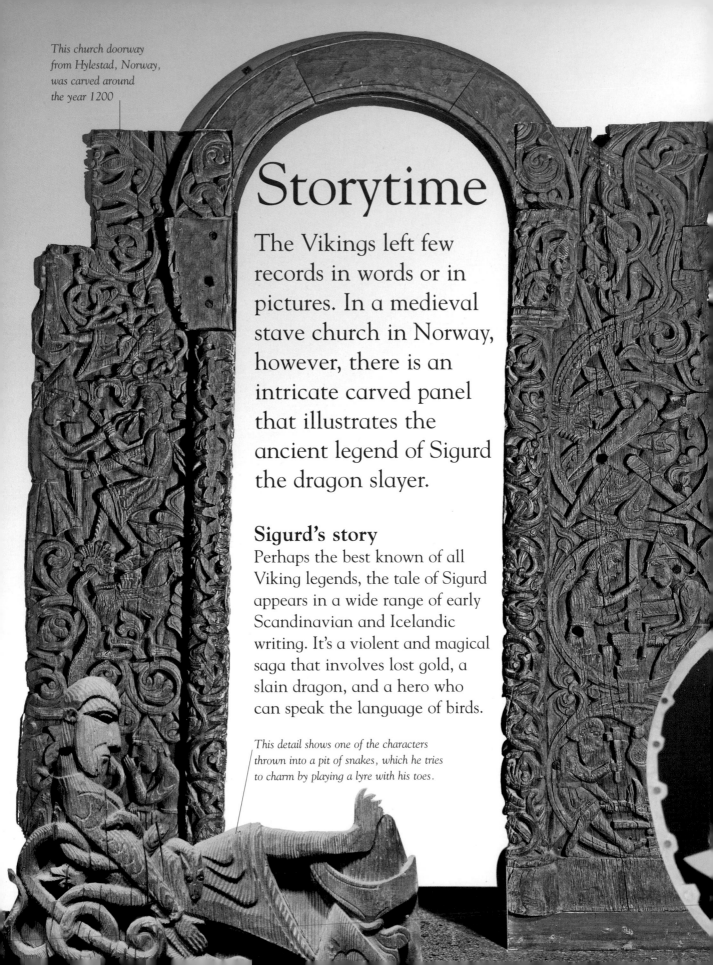

This church doorway
from Hylestad, Norway,
was carved around
the year 1200

# Storytime

The Vikings left few
records in words or in
pictures. In a medieval
stave church in Norway,
however, there is an
intricate carved panel
that illustrates the
ancient legend of Sigurd
the dragon slayer.

## Sigurd's story

Perhaps the best known of all
Viking legends, the tale of Sigurd
appears in a wide range of early
Scandinavian and Icelandic
writing. It's a violent and magical
saga that involves lost gold, a
slain dragon, and a hero who
can speak the language of birds.

*This detail shows one of the characters
thrown into a pit of snakes, which he tries
to charm by playing a lyre with his toes.*

## Thrilling sagas

Skalds were Norse poets who wrote and recited stories of adventure and bravery. These spoken stories usually involved battles between good and evil, and noble warriors who conquered far-off lands and brought home treasure. Often, they married the daughters of kings, reigned over lands, and had large families.

## Magical beasts

Snakes were common in Viking lands and they featured in sagas and poetry, as did mythical creatures such as dragons. This detail from a door on the Oslo City Hall in Norway shows a Viking warrior fighting a snake.

*This replica casket is engraved with mythical animals.*

*Here, Sigurd sucks his thumb while he cooks the heart of the slain dragon.*

## Sharing stories

Instead of writing them down, the Vikings learnt their stories by heart and passed them down from father to son. They believed that their all-powerful god Odin gave them a gift for storytelling.

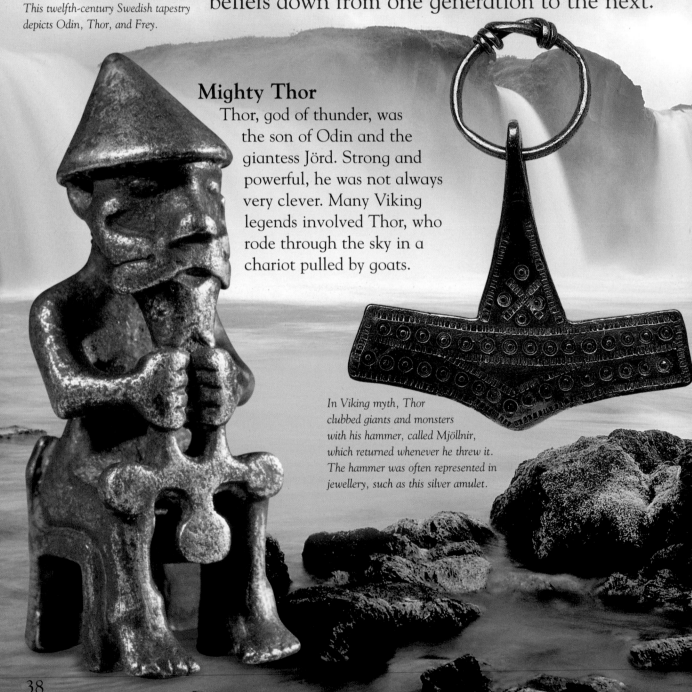

# Legends and beliefs

Before Christianity arrived, Vikings believed in gods like Odin (father of the gods), Thor (god of thunder), and Frey (god of fertility). People made lots of figures of their gods, worshipped them outdoors, and passed their beliefs down from one generation to the next.

*This twelfth-century Swedish tapestry depicts Odin, Thor, and Frey.*

## Mighty Thor

Thor, god of thunder, was the son of Odin and the giantess Jörd. Strong and powerful, he was not always very clever. Many Viking legends involved Thor, who rode through the sky in a chariot pulled by goats.

*In Viking myth, Thor clubbed giants and monsters with his hammer, called Mjöllnir, which returned whenever he threw it. The hammer was often represented in jewellery, such as this silver amulet.*

## Sacred water

Vikings worshipped at the Godafoss waterfall in Iceland (below). Its name means "waterfall of the gods".

### THE NOT-SO-FRIENDLY GIANT

According to myth, a giant called Thrym stole Thor's hammer, and would only give it back if he could marry the goddess Freyja. Thor agreed and dressed up as Freyja for the wedding. When Thrym used the hammer to bless the bride, Thor grabbed it and killed Thrym and all the other giants there.

## Going to glory

Vikings called their heaven Valhalla. The engraving on this stone shows a warrior hero entering Valhalla in triumph.

## Loving gods

Vikings called on Frey to bless their marriages. Legends tell that his sister Freyja, goddess of love and beauty, married the mysterious god Odin, who disappeared soon after. She cried for him and her tears turned to gold.

## Supreme being

The great god Odin was responsible for mystery, poetry, wisdom, and war. All those who died in battle were believed to become sons of Odin.

# Viking burials

Before they converted to Christianity, Vikings were buried with supplies and possessions for the afterlife – everything from clothes, cooking equipment, and furniture to animals and even servants.

*This view of the restored Oseberg ship reveals its graceful curved shape.*

*One of three mysterious dragon-head posts from the Oseberg burial*

### The Oseberg ship
Long preserved in the deep clay of a Norwegian fjord, the Oseberg ship was actually a Viking burial chamber. It was too frail to have sailed the open sea.

### Hidden treasure
Decorated with iron bands and the nails that secure them, this oak tool chest was found in the Oseberg ship when it was discovered in 1903.

## Bridle finery

This section of a horse's bridle was found in the grave of a rich man.

## In honour

This monument at Jelling, Denmark, was built by King Harald Bluetooth as a memorial to his parents (see page 42).

*Engraved silver cup found near the Jelling burial mound*

## Ships of stone

Poor Vikings were never buried in ships, but many decorated their grave sites with raised stones laid out in the shape of a ship.

# Written in stone

Unlike other ancient cultures, the Vikings didn't write on paper, or on anything that was like paper. Almost all their pictures and records were carved in stone, or sometimes in wood. The letters in their alphabet (called runes) were straight and simple, so they could be carved easily.

## Timeless shapes

Using simple tools and specialist knowledge and skill, a present-day stone cutter attempts to re-create an elaborately carved Viking monument.

*This reconstruction of the Jelling stone displays one of the two sides with carved pictures: this one shows mythical beasts.*

*The pictures would originally have been brightly painted.*

*Viking graffiti*

## Ancient graffiti

During his travels through Greece, a Viking traveller carved runes on this stone lion in the Greek port of Piraeus.

*Ribbon shapes form a border around the carved inscription.*

## Memorial stone

Raised by King Harald Bluetooth as a monument to his parents, this great stone is at the royal burial site of Jelling in Denmark. One of the three sides of the stone is covered in runes.

Giant    Torch    Year    Sun  Thor    Water

f   u  th  a  r  k   h  n  i  a  s  t  b  m  l  r

## A, b, c = f, u, th

Runes varied slightly from region to region, but the most common runic alphabet is known as *futhark* after the first three characters (*th* is one character). As well as being letters, each of these represented a word, such as "year" or "sun".

*Runes were thought to have magical properties. Carved onto small stones, they were used to tell future, heal the sick, and bless people, places, and objects.*

*Vikings kept fine combs in cases to protect them.*

## Standing stones

More than 3,000 Viking rune stones have been discovered – mostly in Scandinavia, but also in the rest of Europe. This one is a monument to a Danish king who died in the 10th century.

## Proud owner

In everyday life, the Vikings didn't use runes to tell stories, but for practical purposes, such as labelling objects. This comb case carries the inscription "Thorfast made a good comb". Engraved on weapons, runes were thought to enhance their power in battle.

# The coming of Christianity

Viking raiders and traders came across Christian beliefs throughout Europe. It took them a while to embrace the new faith. Some were only persuaded when they saw that Christian missionaries and kings were not struck down by Viking gods.

*Stave church (made from wooden planks) in the Folk Museum in Oslo, Norway*

*Wooden crosses decorate the portals.*

## Cross for protection

Viking traders often wore a cross so they could travel easily through Christian countries. This cross is from Birka in Uppland, Sweden.

*The Vikings retained traces of their beliefs. The dragon heads that adorn the gables of this church are inspired by Viking mythology.*

## Buildings and burials

When the Vikings became Christians, they built churches all over Scandinavia. Christian Vikings also stopped burying the dead with their possessions, and adopted simpler Christian burials.

Soapstone mould from Himmerland in Denmark

Thor's hammer

## Hammers and crosses

An enterprising craftsman used one mould to make Thor's hammer and the Christian cross. Many Christian Vikings held onto a belief in Thor as a kind of religious backup.

Christian cross

## Early Easter eggs

This beautifully decorated egg represents Christ's resurrection from the grave. It may have been brought to the Vikings in Sweden by Russian missionaries.

Resurrection egg made in Russia

## Saint Ansgar

These carvings, found in a church in Sweden, show Saint Ansgar bringing Christianity to Scandinavia. He was invited by the Swedish king Björn to set up a church.

*This illustration shows a statue of the Viking god Thor being destroyed. King Olaf II Haraldsson converted his people by showing them Thor was powerless.*

Crucifix carved from oak and gilded with copper

## Christ the King

Christ is shown as a king with a crown in this Danish representation of the Crucifixion. Only Christ's hands are nailed to the cross and he looks victorious.

## Kings and Christianity

In Norway, King Olaf II Haraldsson made his people adopt Christian beliefs. He saw Christianity as a way of strengthening his control of the kingdom by emphasizing the rule of law rather than the power of the sword.

# On a quest

A Viking ship is sailing in search of a new colony to settle. Help it find the way by answering the questions correctly.

"sea raider

The word "Viking" means...
**See page 4**

"sea monster"

ropes

Ship's oars were held in place by...
**See page 7**

iron chains

leather straps

Greenland

iron plates

Newfoundland

Erik the Red fled from...
**See page 8**

START

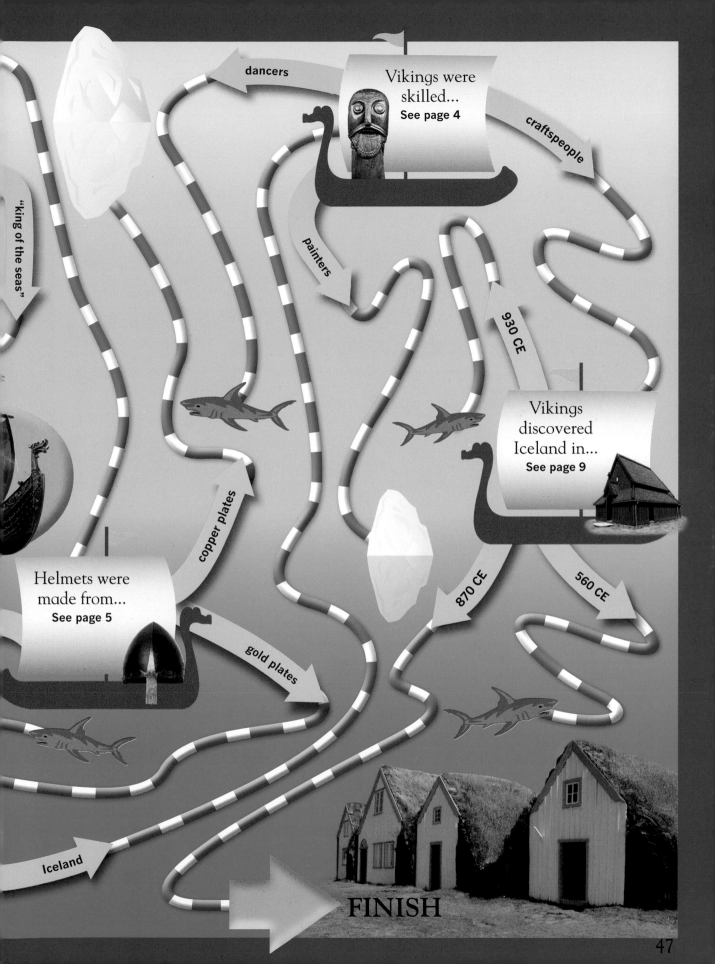

dancers

Vikings were skilled...
See page 4

craftspeople

"king of the seas"

painters

930 CE

Vikings discovered Iceland in...
See page 9

copper plates

Helmets were made from...
See page 5

870 CE

560 CE

gold plates

Iceland

FINISH

# True or false?

It's time to test your knowledge about Vikings. Spot whether these statements are true or false. Have a go!

**Valuables** were kept locked in cupboards.
**See page 17**

**Thor's weapon,** a spear, was often shown in jewellery.
**See page 38**

Shoes, belts, and clothing were made of **leather**.
**See page 26**

Vikings frightened enemies with **ferocious figureheads.**
**See page 7**

For **navigation,** Vikings used a compass.
**See page 6**

Vikings played **board games** scratched onto wood.
**See page 34**

**Horizontal looms** were used to weave cloth.
**See page 26**

**Jewellery** displayed a Viking's status.
**See page 20**

**Young boys** played with real weapons made of iron.
**See page 32**

**Vikings** buried their dead with supplies – including furniture.
**See page 40**

**Able warriors** got land and riches as rewards.
**See page 13**

# Journey home

A tired Viking warrior is returning home. Help him to overcome the obstacles in his path and reach his family.

Slow down to steal some silver. **Go back 4**

Wear ice skates. **Move forward 3**

Rest in the shade of a tree. **Miss a go**

Cross a river on a ferry. **Move forward 3**

Fight with enemies. **Miss a go**

## How to play

This game is for up to four players.

**Move down**   **Move up**

**You will need**
- A dice
- Counters – one for each player

Trace over the helmet outlines, or cut and colour your own from card. Each player takes turns to throw the dice, and begins from the START box. Follow the squares with each roll of the dice. If you land on an instruction, make sure you do as it says. Good luck!

## START

Use a rune as a charm. **Move forward 2**

FINISH
**You have finally reached home!**

Volcano erupts! **Miss a go**

Find an extra bag of coins. **Move forward 3**

Look for your lost gold rings. **Go back 5**

Mountain range blocks the way. **Go back 2**

Hunt for deer. **Go back 4**

Get energy from fruits. **Move forward 2**

# Facts match

How well do you know the Vikings? Read the clues and see if you can match them with the correct pictures.

Etched pendant

Silver and glass cups

Glass beads

Jewellery

Chain mail

This was used for cooking food over a fire. **See page 25**

Musicians played this in rich Viking households while stories were told. **See page 35**

These letters were thought to have magical properties. **See page 43**

Viking traders often wore items such as this while they travelled through Christian countries. **See page 44**

This was found near the Jelling burial mound. **See page 41**

Made of woven branches, this formed the basic structure of Viking houses. **See page 17**

These were built to navigate shallow waters and land on flat shorelines. **See page 11**

Longship

Vikings used these to weigh silver and other precious metals. **See page 29**

This protective tunic is woven from iron links. **See page 19**

**Silver cup**

**Harp**

**Wattle**

**Duck**

**Scales**

**Peasant**

**Cross**

**Runes**

**Coins**

**Cauldron**

**Sword**

**Brooch**

This piece of jewellery was made from a pressed sheet of gold. **See page 20**

This was used for hand-to-hand combat. Wealthy Vikings often had the hilt, or handle, decorated. **See page 15**

Made from glass, these were considered valuable. **See page 21**

This jewellery was inspired by the mythological story of Thor and takes its shape from his weapon. **See page 20**

These were made in large quantities under King Harald Bluetooth. **See page 29**

Rich Vikings drank from these as well as from drinking horns. **See page 31**

These were caught in traps or hunted with short arrows. **See page 25**

Somebody from this rank would have no protective clothing if called to war. **See page 19**

Both male and female Vikings wore these on their fingers, arms, and neck. **See page 21**

# Glossary

Here are the meanings of some words that are useful
to know when you're learning about Vikings.

**baldric** leather strap worn across the body to hold a sword.

**barbarian** coarse, wild, or uncultured person. Vikings were thought to be barbarians.

**boss** knob or stud that sticks out. Viking shields had bosses.

**bow** prow (or front) of a ship (opposite of **stern**).

**casket** small box or chest, often decorated, that holds valuables or religious relics.

**cauldron** large iron or stone cooking pot that Vikings hung over a fire.

**chain mail** flexible, protective armour made from tiny iron rings linked together almost like knitting.

**daub** clay or dung plastered over **wattle** to make walls or fences.

**figurehead** ornamental carving on the prow of a ship.

**fjord** long, thin, finger-shaped body of water that extends inland from an ocean or sea, often between high cliffs.

**futhark** a basic early Scandinavian alphabet named after its first six letters. (*See also* **rune**)

**guard** metal collar between the blade of a sword and its handle, which protects the user's hand.

**hack silver** chopped-up bits of jewellery and coins that was used as money.

**hilt** the handle of a sword or a dagger.

**hneftafl** Viking game played with wooden counters on a wooden or leather board.

**hoard** stash of buried Viking treasure, which could include jewellery, coins, or anything else made from precious metal.

**hull** body or frame of a ship.

**jarl** earl, noble, or chieftain; one of the three classes in Viking society. (*See also* **karl**, **thrall**)

**karl** freeman (not slave); largest of the three classes in Viking society. (*See also* **jarl**, **thrall**)

**keel** long section of timber that extends along the base of a ship from prow to stern. A ship's framework is built on its keel.

**longship** ship powered by lines of rowers as well as by one rectangular sail.

**mast** timber or iron pole that supports a ship's sail.

**missionary** a person who tries to convert someone else to a different faith from the one they believe in.

**New World** mainly used to refer to North and South America, which were unfamiliar to ancient people.

**niello** black metallic compound of sulphur with silver, lead, or copper used for decoration in silver etc.

**plunder** to take goods by force. The Vikings plundered villages, farms, and churches wherever they travelled.

**prow** front section of a ship or boat (opposite of **stern**).

**quern** small round stone for grinding wheat into flour.

**rampart** mound of earth and turf supported on a wooden framework. Ramparts were used for defence.

**rigging** arrangement of a ship's mast, sails, rope, etc.

**runes** early Scandinavian letters based on Greek and Roman characters, but simplified to make them easier to carve.

**skald** Viking entertainer who wrote and recited stories in poetry form about kings, battles, and heroes.

**sledge** flat surface on runners. People travelled on sledges, but they were also used to carry heavy loads.

**smith** someone who works with metal, such as a goldsmith, a silversmith, or a tinsmith. Blacksmiths work with iron.

**spindle** small rod with tapered ends used in spinning for twisting and winding yarn.

**stave** upright wooden plank, post, or log used in the construction of buildings.

**stern** rear section of a ship (opposite of **bow** or **prow**).

**sternpost** ornamental carving on the stern of a ship.

**Thing** local assembly. All freemen could express opinions at their Thing.

**thrall** Viking slave. A slave is a person who is owned by another person, usually for the purpose of doing some kind of work; one of the three classes in Viking society. (*See also* **jarl**, **karl**)

**trefoil** three-lobed shape that was popular in the design of Viking jewellery, particularly brooches.

**wattle** woven branches used to form the framework of wattle-and-daub walls and fences. (*See also* **daub**)

*Viking burial site in Sweden*

# Index

## Acknowledgements

**Dorling Kindersley would like to thank:**
Dave Thirlwall at the Murton Park Viking village, York, UK; Alicia Anderson, Max Bongart, Dave Elliott, Jill Moore, Duncan Morris-Metcalf, Victoria Midda, Kay Newman, Rebbecca Pateman, Susan Rawlings, Rebecca and Sophie Scott, John and Fenn Lomax Shulver, Doreen and Peter Smith, Mick Suffolk, Andrew, Fayth, Kerri, and Wyatt Thomas, Bruce Tordoff, Paulina and Stanislaw Wdowczyk, Jane Wheatley, and Alison Wood for modelling; Andy Cooke for artwork; Iorwerth Watkins for cartography; Hedi Gutt and Siamak Tannazi for photographic assistance; and Anna and Martin Edmondson for location assistance. DK would also like to thank Fleur Star and Caroline Bingham for proof-reading.

## Picture credits

**The publisher would like to thank the following for their kind permission to reproduce their photographs:**
(Key: a-above; b-below/bottom; c-centre; l-left; r-right; t-top)
**Alamy Images:** Daniel Bergmann 38-39 (background); Mandy Collins 12-13br; Danita Delimont 37t; Bernie Epstein 7tr; David R Frazier 23t; Les Gibbon 22cr; Leslie Garland Picture Library 43br; Mary Evans Picture Library 45bl; David Muenker 17cl; Kari Niemeläinen 15tr, 30bl, 35br; Nordic Photos 2-3; Pixonnet.com 42ca; Robert Harding Picture Library 9tc, 40tr; Stefan Sollfors 42-43tr; Doug Steley 37bl; Visual Arts Library 38bl; Scott Carruthers 49b; **Archeon.nl:** 27; **Jon Arnold:** Walter Bibikow 54-55; **The Bridgeman Art Library:** Bibliotheque des Arts Decoratifs, Paris, France / Archives Charmet 29tr; National Museum of Scotland 28c; **Danny Cambré:** 32tc; **Dick Clark:** Dick Clark 26bc; **Corbis:** Stefano Bianchetti 11tr; Christophe Boisvieux 41r; Wolfgang Kaehler 16t; Charles & Josette Lenars 32bc; Buddy Mays 28l; Ted Spiegel 8tl, 10tl, 31t; Stapleton Collection 45tr; Werner Forman 9cr, 36b, 37br, 37cra, 38t; Yadid Levy / Robert Harding World Imagery 46bc; **Dorling Kindersley:** British Museum, London 15cra, 21cb, 21crb, 23cr, 24clb, 29ca, 29clb, 29tl, 56t; Danish National Museum 12bl, 12clb, 13tl, 17cr, 20bl, 20c, 21bl, 21tl, 24bl, 31cl, 34ca, 38cr, 41bl, 42cr, 43ca, 43clb, 45bc; Natural History Museum, London 25tc; Roskilde Viking Ships Museum, Denmark 7cla; Statens Historiska Museum, Stockholm 4tl, 20tr, 29bc, 31cr, 35bl, 35cl, 39c, 39l, 41tl, 45cl; Universitetets kulturhistoriske museer/ Vikingskipshuset 7tc; Universitets Oldsaksamling, Oslo 26cl, 31bc, 36t, 40cr, 40l; Yorkshire Museum 22tl, 26cr, 34cra, 34crb; Cecil Williamson Collection 53clb (Rusty cauldron), 58bl; Danish National Museum 48c, 53bl, 58ca (bronze key), Peter Hanneberg 59bl, The Museum of London 58c, 58bc, The National Music Museum 53tc (Harp), Natural History Museum, London 59crb (Amber), Roskilde Viking Ships Museum, Denmark 46clb, 50clb, 58bc (Steering oar), Rough Guides 2bc, 47cr, Statens Historiska Museum, Stockholm 52tc, 52tr, 52tr (Byzantine silver cup.), 58c (Statue), 59ca, 59clb, 59cb, 59bc (Bone flute ), Universitetets kulturhistoriske museer / Vikingskipshuset 52br, Universitets Oldsaksamling, Oslo 47cr, Vikings of Middle England 48crb, 50cb, 51cla, 51c, 51clb, 51bc, 53cl, 59crb, 59bc; **Dreamstime.com:** Atu Studio Atu Studio 48br, Paul Fleet 48bl, Michael Flippo 58tl, Mikhail Kokhanchikov 51cra, Aleksander Lorenz 50br, Margo555 51br, Nneiole 47br, Pterwort 53cra, Natalia Sevriukova 59cb (Old brown pitcher), Danny Smythe 46cr, 59br, Torbjörn Swenelius 59ca (quarterstallion), Voltan1 59tc; **Flickr.com:** Brian Butler 9br; Stefan Chivers 9cl; Michel Craipeau 7clb; Gunnar Danielson 17tr; Gisele Hannemyr 14-15br; D Prior 15tl; Hans Splinter 23bc, 26bl, 33b; Grant Way 21r; **Fotevikens Museum, Sweden:** 35tl; **Fotolia:** Sascha Burkard 58ca, byrdyak 51bl, Magann 58tc; **Getty Images:** AFP 10-11bc; Walter Bibikow 7br; Per Breiehagen 34 (background); Sisse Brimberg 24tl; Robert Harding World Imagery 10c; Hulton Archive 40br; National Geographic / Ted Spiegel 6b; Nordic Photos 4bc; Jochem Wijnands 56 (background); Danita Delimont / Gallo Images 53tc, Werner Forman / Universal Images Group 53clb; **Carrie Love:** 5br, 15br, 16b, 17br, 17tc, 17tl, 18br, 18c, 18l, 19r, 22cb, 29bl, 30cr, 30-31, 32br, 32tr, 33c, 33tr; **PBase:** Jim Lanyon 35bc; **Reuters:** Kieran Doherty 1; **Scanpix Denmark:** 14c; **Still Pictures:** Markus Dlouhy 31bl; Thomas Haertrich 18cr, 33tl; **TopFoto.co.uk:** 30t; The British Library 6t; The British Museum 10tr; Firth 24-25b; **Gary Waidson:** 15cl, 35tr; Gary Waidson 26tl; **Werner Forman Archive:** 44b, 45r; British Museum London 11bc, 11bl; National Museum, Copenhagen 45tl; Statens Historiska Museet, Stockholm 11br, 39br; Wikipedia, **The Free Encyclopedia:** Árni Magnússon Institute, Iceland 34bl; Casiopeia 41cl; **York Archaeological Trust:** 28cb

All other images © Dorling Kindersley
**For further information see: www.dkimages.com**